WonderWorks

Decodable Reader

Unit 5

Mc Graw Hill

Contents

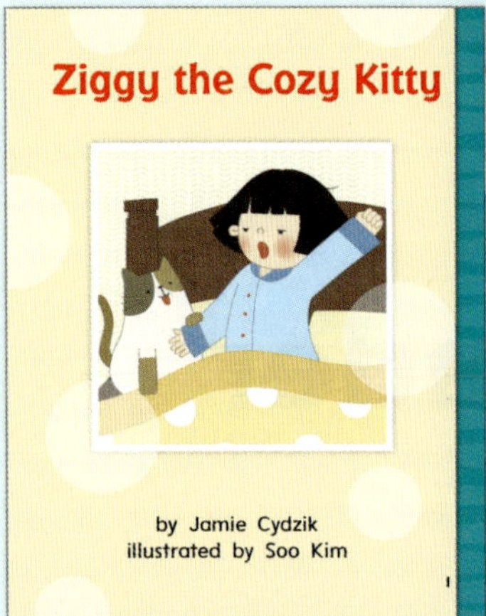

Ziggy the Cozy Kitty
by Jamie Cydzik
illustrated by Soo Kim
1

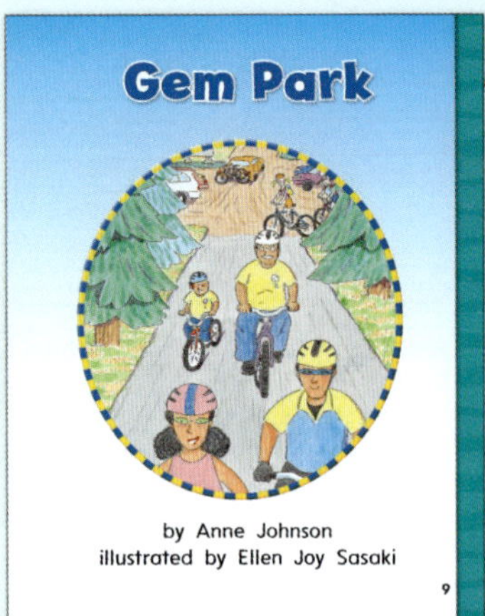

Gem Park
by Anne Johnson
illustrated by Ellen Joy Sasaki
9

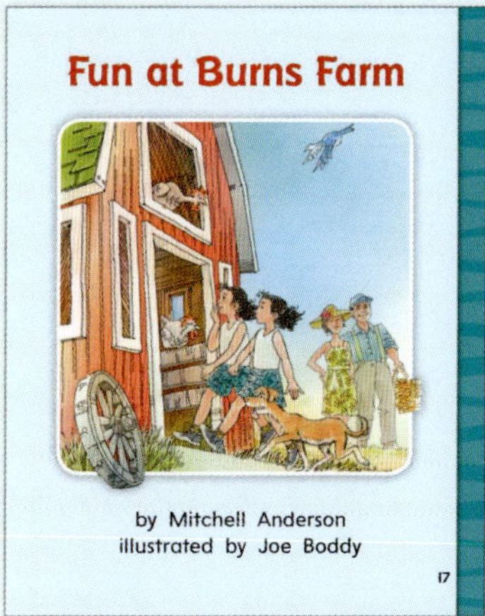
Fun at Burns Farm
by Mitchell Anderson
illustrated by Joe Boddy
17

Work at a Port
by Craig Mellon
25

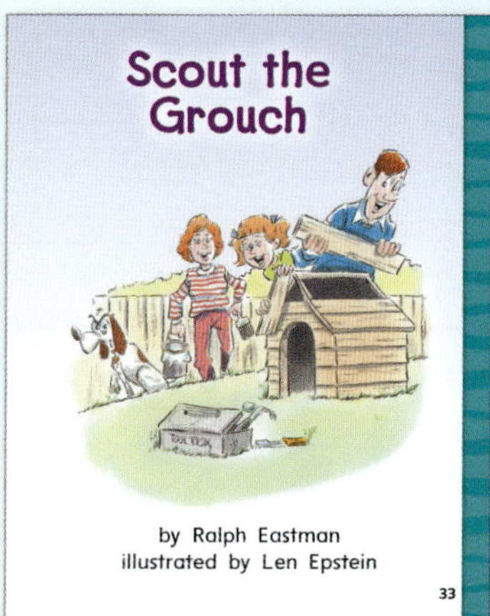
Scout the Grouch
by Ralph Eastman
illustrated by Len Epstein
33

Ziggy the Cozy Kitty

by Jamie Cydzik
illustrated by Soo Kim

It's time to wake up! Lily is still sleepy in bed. Ziggy the tiny kitty is ready to go out!

Lily and Ziggy look. No! It is misty and windy outside.
"It's too muggy, Ziggy."
They see a man and **woman** in the yucky rain.

Ziggy is fussy and cranky. He wants to go!

"We can have fun inside too," says Lily.

She knows it isn't **hard** to make Ziggy happy.

"**Would** you like a yummy snack?" asks Lily.
Ziggy gets peppy. He has a full tummy. Yum!

"We can sketch and **write**," Lily says.

Ziggy comes **near** Lily. She rubs his fuzzy belly. Ziggy **found** a cozy spot.

“Look, Ziggy! It is sunny!”
But the silly kitty is too sleepy.
“You are a really funny
buddy, Ziggy. And I am
really lucky!”

Gem Park

by Anne Johnson
illustrated by Ellen Joy Sasaki

Gem Park is a **large** park.

It has a parking lot for cars.
It has a bike path for bikes.

The pathway is **four** miles. It is **only** for bikes. It is flat at the start. Riding is not hard.

The children **put** on their helmets and ride.

The bike path winds uphill and downhill. This part passes by a cliff. The fence makes it safe so **none** of the bikes will slip off.

Stop at the hilltop and rest a moment. Look far across the land.

A big red barn sits on green farmland.

The path goes by a sharp bend and then starts down a steep hill.

The **round** bike tires go fast.

The bike path ends at this huge rock. Rest and relax. Then you might jump on that bike and take one more lap!

Fun at Burns Farm

by Mitchell Anderson
illustrated by Joe Boddy

Farmer Burns is hosting a picnic. Cars drive **through** his gate. Bert greets each one. Soon the lot is **full** of cars.

Burns Farm has a red barn.
These twin girls enter it.

Will there be baby chicks inside?

They walk on the dirt. The first chick has just hatched. It turns to look at the girls.

They take slow steps so they don't disturb the baby bird.

Farmer Burns has a cart.
Kids **climb** in for a ride.

They ride past the farmer's herd. The **poor** dog can't fit so she runs beside the cart.

This man pays for jam. The seller hands him **another** jar.

Another person sells shirts and hats. This woman gets cash from her purse to pay.

This fun day is over. It is time to go home.

It is worth a visit to Burns Farm. It is a **great** place!

Work at a Port

by Craig Mellon

Jens Kuhfs/Photographer's Choice/Getty Images

Wolfgang Deuter/Photolibrary/Getty Images

Roger Tulley/The Image Bank/GettyImages

A port is a safe place for ships to dock.

What happens at a port? Many jobs get done there.

Jens Kuhfs/Photographer's Choice/Getty Images

A ship is coming in. It **began** its trip days ago. Now it is **sure** to dock **right** on time.

The ship blasts its horn on its way in.

Lisa-Blue/E+/Getty Images

A tugboat meets this ship and leads it to the shore.

It is **better** for tugs to lead the ship in. The ship will be safe that way.

F1 Online/SuperStock

This ship has large crates on board. A crane unloads cargo. Forklift drivers lift more cargo off the ship.

They **learn** to sort it in piles.

Jason Homa/The Image Bank/Getty Images

Cargo is loaded on trucks. The trucks bring the cargo to stores on York Rd.

The drivers use maps. They do not want to **guess** the way.

Wolfgang Deuter/Photolibrary/Getty Images

This ship is empty. It will go pick up more cargo. Then it will drop off its load at the next port.

Scout the Grouch

by Ralph Eastman
illustrated by Len Epstein

Noreen gave her hound plenty of hugs each day. But **nothing** Noreen did made Scout happy.

Scout was a grouch.

Dad, Mom, and Noreen got up **early** to make Scout his own doghouse.

They felt proud of this house. But Scout was still a grouch.

Dad **thought** dog bones might help. He got a pound of bones. He set down the largest bone on the ground. It was the **color** of snow.

Instead of taking the bone, Scout howled. It got louder.

Dad and Noreen tried blocking out these sounds. Scout was still a grouch.

Noreen said, "**Oh**! I know.
How about a nice long run?"
They ran around the park.

Now Scout felt wiped out.
He was a sleepy grouch.

It was time to feed Scout.
Noreen found him napping.
Scout was not frowning!

He had found a mouse pal.
Now Scout was happy.

Unit 5

Word Count: 132

Decodable Words

Target Phonics Element: Long *e* (*y, ey*)
belly, buddy, cozy, cranky, funny, fussy, fuzzy, happy, kitty, Lily, lucky, misty, muggy, peppy, ready, really, silly, sleepy, sunny, tiny, tummy, windy, yucky, yummy, Ziggy
Review: *am, asks, and, bed, but, can, fun, full, gets, he, his, in, inside, is, it, go, like, make, man, no, rain, rubs, see, she, sketch, snack, spot, still, time, up, wake, we, yum*

High-Frequency Words

found, hard, near, woman, would, write
Review: *are, comes, have, knows, out, the, to, too, you*

Word Count: 137

Decodable Words

Target Phonics Element: *r*-Controlled Vowel *ar*
barn, cars, far, farmland, hard, park, parking, part, sharp, start, starts
Review: *a, across, and, at, bend, big, bike, bikes, by, cliff, drink, ends, fast, fence, flat, gem, get, go, goes, green, has, helmets, hill, hilltop, huge, is, it, jump, land, lap, lot, makes, might, miles, moment, not, off, on, passes, path, pathway, red, relax, rest, ride, riding, rock, safe, sits, slip, so, steep, stop, take, that, the, then, this, tires, uphill, will, winds*

High-Frequency Words

four, large, none, only, put, round
Review: *children, down, downhill, for, look, more, of, one, put, their, you*

Word Count: 150

Decodable Words

Target Phonics Element: *r*-Controlled Vowels *er, ir, ur, or*
Bert, bird, Burns, dirt, disturb, farmer, farmer's, first, girls, herd, person, purse, seller, shirts, turns, worth
Review: *a, and, at, baby, barn, be, beside, can't, cars, cart, cash, chick, chicks, day, dog, don't, drive, each, enter, farm, fit, fun, gate, gets, greets, hands, has, hatched, hats, her, him, his, home, hosting, inside, in, is, it, it's, jam, jar, just, kids, lot, man, on, past, pay, pays, picnic, place, red, ride, runs, sells, she, slow, steps, so, take, the, these, this, time, twin, visit, will*

High-Frequency Words

another, climb, full, great, poor, through
Review: *for, from, look, of, over, soon, there, they, to, walk, woman*

Word Count: 161

Decodable Words

Target Phonics Element: *r*-Controlled Vowels *or, ore, oar*
board, forklift, horn, more, or, port, shore, stores, York
Review: *a, ago, and, at, be, big, blasts, boxes, bring, cargo, crane, crates, day, dock, drivers, drop, for, each,*

empty, get, go, happens, has, in, is, it, its, jobs, large, lead, leave, lift, load, loaded, maps, meet, must, next, not, off, on, or, pick, place, safe, ship, ships, so, tells, that, the, then, this, tie, time, trailer, trip, truck, trucks, tugboats, tugs, unload, up, use, waiting, way, will, work

High-Frequency Words

began, better, guess, learn, right, sure
Review: *coming, done, have, many, now, of, other, out, there, they, to, what*

Week 5 • *Scout the Grouch* .... page 33

Word Count: 148

Decodable Words

Target Phonics Element: Diphthongs *ou, ow*
about, around, doghouse, down, found, frowning, grouch, ground, hound, house, how, howled, louder, mouse, now, out, pound, proud, Scout, sounds
Review: *a, and, blocking, bone, bones, but, dad, day, did, dog, each, feed, felt, gave, got, had, happy, he, help, her, him, his, hugs, I, it, know, largest, long, made, make, might, Mom, napping, nice, Noreen, not, on, own, pal, park, plenty, run, set, sleepy, snow, still, taking, the, these, this, time, tried, up, wiped*

High-Frequency Words

color, early, instead, nothing, oh, thought
Review: *of, said, they, to, was*

Decoding skills taught to date:

Phonics: Consonants/Letter Recognition; Short *a*; Short *i*; *l*-Blends; Short *o*; *r*-Blends, *s*-Blends; Short *e* (*e, ea*); Short *u*; End Blends *nd, nk, nt, st, sk, mp*; Consonant Digraphs: *th, sh, -ng*; Consonant Digraphs *ch, -tch, wh, ph*; Long *a (a_e)*; Long *i (i_e)*; Soft *c*; Soft *g, dge*; Long *o (o_e)*; Long *u (u_e)*; Long *e (e_e)*; Variant Vowel /u̇/: *oo, u*; Long *a (a, ai, ay)*; Long *e (e, ee, ea, ie)*; Long *o (o, oa, ow, oe)*; Long *i (i, y, igh, ie)*; Long *e (y, ey)*; *r*-Controlled Vowel *ar*; *r*-Controlled Vowels *er, ir, ur, or;* *r*-Controlled Vowels *or, ore, oar*; Diphthongs *ou, ow*

Structural Analysis: Consonants; Inflectional Ending -*s* (plurals, verbs); Double Final Consonants; Alphabetical Order; Possessives with '*s*; Inflectional Ending -*ed*; Contractions with '*s*; Inflectional Ending -*ing*; Closed Syllables; Inflectional Ending -*es*; Contractions with *n't*; Plurals with CVC*e* Words; Inflectional Endings -*ed, -ing* with Spelling Changes; CVC*e* Syllables; Inflectional Endings -*ed, -ing* Double Final Consonant; Alphabetical Order (two letters); Prefixes *re-, un-, pre-*; Open Syllables; Inflectional Endings Change *y* to *i*; Compound Words; Plurals (irregular); Inflectional Ending -*er*; Abbreviations; Comparative Inflectional Endings -*er, -est*

Check out this car. It has streaks of dirt all over. How can it get clean?

Have you **heard** of a car wash?

Thinkstock/Comstock Images/Getty Images

Take **your** car to get washed. It can be a thrill.

The **front** of the car is first. Then get the wheels on the track and see it get clean.

Jupiterimages/Comstock Images/Getty Images

First, jets of water spray to get the car wet. Then soap squirts out. The car passes through long soft strips of cloth. The strips spread soap on the car.

Jupiterimages/Comstock Images/Getty Images

The car keeps rolling on the track. Water and soap splash on it to scrub off the dirt.

Then more jets stream fresh water on the car.

Thinkstock/Comstock Images/Getty Images

The car passes through a big dryer **before** it leaves the tunnel.

At the end, it gets a **push** out of the tunnel.

Jupiterimages/Comstock Images/Getty Images

The car shines like new. **Tomorrow** it may get dirty again. Then it's back to the car wash!

Unit 6

Word Count: 144

Decodable Words

Target Phonics Element: Diphthongs *oy, oi*
avoid, coins, Floyd, foil, joined, Joy, Joyce, pointed, spoiled, soil, voice
Review: *a, an, and, at, back, bright, candy, closer, coast, crashed, filled, find, gazed, go, gold, had, happy, he, help, hike, hiked, huddled, I, I'll, in, it, it's, just, keep, let's, lighthouse, lighthouses, look, looked, looking, loud, made, maybe, noise, not, on, paper, rain, rainbow, rocks, sandy, she, shelter, shiny, ship, ships, slip, smiled, sunk, stopped, that, that's, the, them, then, thing, those, told, tried, up, us, waves, we, will, with*

High-Frequency Words

above, build, fall, knew, money, toward
Review: *called, of, old, said, thought, to, under, walked, was, water, why*

Word Count: 146

Decodable Words

Target Phonics Element: Variant Vowel /ü/: *oo, u, u_e, ew, ue, ui, ou*
blooms, chew, cool, coop, dew, blue, Bruce, few, food, fruit, June, loons, Luke, moo, mood, new, poof, Ruth, scoops, soon, Sue, wooly, you, zoom
Review: *bright, by, checked, checks, chicks, cow, day, each, farm, feels, fixing, fresh, good, grass, has, help, hen, hot, in, is, likes, morning, no, on, pig, place, pond, pretty, pup, rests, sees, she, sheep, sky, spots, squints, start, stay, Sun, time, up, waves, will, yum*

High-Frequency Words

answer, brought, busy, door, enough, eyes
Review: *friends, of, the, there, they, to, water, your*

Word Count: 164

Decodable Words

Target Phonics Element: Variant Vowel /ô/: *a, aw, au, augh, al*
awful, awning, because, cawed, crawled, dawn, halt, hawk, lawn, paused, saw, small, tall, taught, squawked, wanted
Review: *a, about, and, around, at, away, beak, bird, birds, book, bugs, bunting, buntings, but, came, car, day, did, didn't, driveway, fast, felt, five, flew, food, for, gave, go, good, got, grass, home, I, in, is, it, it's, itchy, looking, matter, maybe, me, morning, my, no, not, on, out, sad, see, short, spot, spotted, tail, that, the, them, things, this, time, up, wake, walked, when, with, wood*

High-Frequency Words

brother, father, friend, love, mother, picture
Review: *another, knew, love, many, of, one, they, to, two, was*

Word Count: 158

Decodable Words

Target Phonics Element: Silent Letters *wr, kn, gn*
gnashed, knapsack, knee, knew, knife, knight, knight's, knit, knocked, knot, know, Knox, wrong, wrote
Review: *a, all, along, and, ask, asked, bed, being, bread, but, butter, by, can, each, farm, for, got, he, his, homemade,*

how, I, is, it, job, kind, king, left, let, me, no, note, on, packed, passed, perform, pile, quit, sharpen, sheep, smiled, socks, soft, started, task, teeth, the, then, this, tie, time, use, Waldo, wool, you

Review: *do, doing, done, door, have, into, said, their, to, together, was, what*

High-Frequency Words

been, children, month, question, their, year

Week 5 • *Scrubbing Cars Clean*......................page 33

Word Count: 156

Decodable Words

Target Phonics Elements: Three-Letter Blends *scr, spl, spr, str, thr*

scrub, scrubbing, splash, spray, spread, streaks, stream, strips, thrill

Review: *a, all, and, as, at, back, big, by, can, car, cars, car wash, check, clean, cleaned, cloth, dirt, dirty, dryer, end, fast, first, forth, get, gets, go, hand, has, how, in, is, it, it's, jets, leaves, like, line, lot, may, mess, more, off, on, new, out, over, passes, pay, push, rinse, rolling, rolls, sit, soap, soft, sparkles, spin, squirts, takes, that, the, then, these, this, time, track, tunnel, wet, will, you*

High-Frequency Words

before, front, heard, push, tomorrow, your

Review: *again, have, money, move, of, they, through, to, water*

Decoding skills taught to date:

Phonics: Consonants/Letter Recognition; Short *a;* Short *i;* *l*-Blends; Short *o;* *r*-Blends, *s*-Blends; Short *e (e, ea);* Short *u;* End Blends *nd, nk, nt, st, sk, mp;* Consonant Digraphs: *th, sh, -ng;* Consonant Digraphs *ch, -tch, wh, ph;* Long *a (a_e);* Long *i (i_e);* Soft *c;* Soft *g, dge;* Long *o (o_e);* Long *u (u_e);* Long *e (e_e);* Variant Vowel /ů/: *oo, u;* Long *a (a, ai, ay);* Long *e (e, ee, ea, ie);* Long *o (o, oa, ow, oe);* Long *i (i, y, igh, ie);* Long *e (y, ey);* *r*-Controlled Vowel *ar;* *r*-Controlled Vowels *er, ir, ur, or;* *r*-Controlled Vowels *or, ore, oar;* Diphthongs *ou, ow;* Diphthongs *oy, oi;* Variant Vowel /ü/: *oo, u, u_e, ew, ue, ui, ou;* Variant Vowel /ô/: a, *aw, au, augh, al;* Silent Letters *wr, kn, gn;* Three-Letter Blends *scr, spl, spr, str, thr, shr*

Structural Analysis: Consonants; Inflectional Ending *-s* (plurals, verbs); Double Final Consonants; Alphabetical Order; Possessives with *'s;* Inflectional Ending *-ed;* Contractions with *'s;* Inflectional Ending *-ing;* Closed Syllables; Inflectional Ending *-es;* Contractions with *n't;* Plurals with CVC*e* Words; Inflectional Endings *-ed, -ing* with Spelling Changes; CVC*e* Syllables; Inflectional Endings *-ed, -ing;* Double Final Consonant; Alphabetical Order (two letters); Prefixes *re-, un-, pre-;* Open Syllables; Inflectional Endings Change *y* to *i;* Compound Words; Plurals (irregular); Inflectional Ending *-er;* Abbreviations; Comparative Inflectional Endings *-er, -est;* Final Stable Syllables; Suffixes *-ful* and *-less;* Vowel Team Syllables; Compound Words; Inflectional Endings *-ed, -ing*